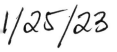

The Eating Disorder Recovery Journal

The Eating Disorder Recovery Journal

CARA LISETTE

Foreword by Dr Emily David
Illustrated by Victoria Barron

Jessica Kingsley Publishers
London and Philadelphia

First published in Great Britain in 2022 by Jessica Kingsley Publishers
An imprint of Hodder & Stoughton Ltd
An Hachette Company

1

A CIP catalogue record for this title is available from the
British Library and the Library of Congress

ISBN 978 1 83997 085 6
eISBN 978 1 83997 086 3

Printed and bound in Great Britain by Bell & Bain Limited

Jessica Kingsley Publishers' policy is to use papers that are natural, renewable and recyclable
products and made from wood grown in sustainable forests. The logging and manufacturing
processes are expected to conform to the environmental regulations of the country of origin.

Jessica Kingsley Publishers
Carmelite House
50 Victoria Embankment
London EC4Y 0DZ

www.jkp.com

Foreword

Life with an eating disorder can be overwhelming, all-consuming and exhausting. It sucks the fun and joy out of life. If you have picked up this recovery journal you will know this only too well.

You do not deserve this eating disorder.

It is not your fault.

It is not a choice.

Despite this, there are choices that can be made when it comes to recovery. Choices that can help you take a step closer to recovery and the goals you want to achieve, whatever this looks like and whatever these are for you. Those steps might seem terrifying and difficult to make, but by picking up this recovery journal you're making a positive choice and step towards your recovery goals. Cara's recovery journal is jam packed full of heartfelt, tried and tested and useful approaches, techniques, ideas and exercises to help you reflect on where you are right now, where you want to get to and the changes you'll need to make in order to get there. Even more importantly, this journal will help inspire and motivate you to bring fun and joy back into your life – to make life worth living, free of your eating disorder.

No two people with an eating disorder are the same. Different things connect, inspire and help different people. The beauty of this journal is that it can help anyone – at any stage of their recovery journey – and it will be completely unique to you. With so many different things to try, you are bound to find things that stick in your mind, that motivate you or encourage you to take steps towards achieving your goals. Even on your most wobbly of days when you feel like giving up, this journal will hopefully help you navigate those thoughts and feelings. Many of the techniques and approaches in this journal are ones that I use and share with people I work with, and I am looking forward to being able to share this journal with them as a useful tool. Once you have completed it, my top tip would be to keep it somewhere safe and refer back to it regularly as it will help you to stay on track.

Recovery isn't easy; it's one of the hardest things you'll ever do. It takes effort, commitment and persistence. Recovery is possible and most definitely worth it.

Cara did it and so can you.

Sending you strength in your recovery journey and I hope you find the joy in life once again,

Emily

Dr Emily David
Clinical Psychologist

Hello, warrior!

Welcome to your eating disorder recovery journal. Throughout this book there are a number of exercises to help you to explore your eating disorder and motivate you through your recovery journey.

This is your book to use as you choose: you can write in it, draw in it, decorate it – in any way you like. Creativity is an excellent outlet and I hope you find that some of these prompts bring you closer to your goals. There is no particular order or time frame to complete this journal in – you can do it at your own pace and use each exercise as little or often as you find helpful.

I created this journal based on my own experiences of living with an eating disorder and my subsequent recovery journey; the activities included are all things that have helped me to challenge my eating disorder and aid my recovery in its many stages. I hope that you might find some of them as valuable as I have.

I know that it might feel impossible at times, no matter what stage of your journey you are at. Keep fighting; there is so much more to life than living with an eating disorder, and you deserve to recover.

Never forget that you are amazing, you are worthy, and you are enough.

Lots of love, Cara

My recovery goals

Start by setting yourself some goals. What would you like to achieve, and by when?

1. ....
   ....

2. ....
   ....

3. ....
   ....

4. ....
   ....

5. ....
   ....

6. ....
   ....

7. ....
   ....

8. ....
   ....

9. ....
   ....

10. ....
    ....

My reasons to recover

1. I want a healthy relationship with food – balanced mindset/attitude.
2. I want food to bring me joy and be a creative outlet.
3. I don't want food to take up so much headspace.
4. For my future self. And my present self.
5. For my future family.
6.
7.
8.
9.
10.

Recovery poster

It can be really helpful when we are in recovery to have visual aids. It's easy to forget why we are fighting so hard when things feel difficult and sometimes they feel downright impossible.

I like to make myself reminders, and something I have found useful is to write down all the reasons I am recovering and turn it into a poster to put up somewhere. Try making a poster of the list of the reasons you have written down on the previous page and displaying it somewhere that is easy to see at home.

It can also be good to photograph this on your phone so you have it with you when you are out and about.

Recovery mantras

Nothing good will ever come from hating yourself

You are enough

Your body isn't meant to stay at a weight you
can only sustain through restriction

When you starve yourself you feed your eating disorder

Sometimes the fear won't go away, so you have to do it afraid

Your weight does not define you

No food will ever hurt you as much as your eating disorder will

Eating won't kill you – not eating will

Useful distractions

It can be really hard to ignore that eating disorder voice and the urges that come along with it. Here are some suggestions for distractions to help you cope with the anxiety of not acting on those urges.

- Writing
- Drawing
- Reading a book
- Watching a film
- Listening to podcasts or a happy playlist
- Arts and crafts
- Painting your nails
- Having a bath or shower
- Crossword puzzles
- Playing a game
- Colouring books

Distractions that help me

You might already have your own ideas for distraction techniques that help you. Write down some ideas that you could try if you need to take your mind off things.

1. *Movement* ....
   ....

2. ....
   ....

3. ....
   ....

4. ....
   ....

5. ....
   ....

6. ....
   ....

7. ....
   ....

8. ....
   ....

9. ....
   ....

10. ....
   ....

How are you feeling today? Draw or write it out!

Things I like about myself

1. ....
   ....

2. ....
   ....

3. ....
   ....

4. ....
   ....

5. ....
   ....

6. ....
   ....

7. ....
   ....

8. ....
   ....

9. ....
   ....

10. ....
    ....

Quotes, lyrics and phrases that inspire me

Quote jars

Quote jars can be a really helpful way to start the day and keep you motivated. Try writing down on pieces of paper some of the recovery mantras from this book and some of the quotes and lyrics that inspire you personally, then fold them up and put them in a jar. You can take one out every morning, or just whenever you feel like you need a boost of recovery motivation to keep you focussed and on track.

Why do I deserve to eat and recover?

It can be really difficult in recovery to feel like we are deserving, not just of food but of any sort of care or attention. However, you do deserve to nourish yourself and give yourself the best chance at a life free from your eating disorder. Have a think about some of the reasons why.

1. ....
....

2. ....
....

3. ....
....

4. ....
....

5. ....
....

6. ....
....

7. ....
....

8. ....
....

9. ....
....

10. ....
....

Comparing ourselves to others

Comparison is something a lot of people struggle with, but especially those with eating disorders. You might find that you are comparing yourself to other people's bodies, what they are eating and how much they are exercising, among other things.

The most important thing to remember is that we are only seeing a snapshot of other people's lives, both in real life and on social media. You may see somebody eating a smaller lunch than you, but maybe they had a bigger breakfast. You might see somebody on Instagram and wish you looked like them, but even they probably don't look like that photo in real life.

Remember, comparison is the thief of joy.

We are all individuals on different paths with our own bodies, minds and lives. The only person you need to focus on is yourself.

Life is tough but
so are you

Recovery isn't linear

Recovery is rarely a straight line. Remember that setbacks are a normal part of the journey and are not an indicator of failure. Keep going – you've got this.

Brain dump

How are you feeling right now? Sometimes getting our thoughts out onto the page can help us to process and make sense of them.

....

....

....

....

....

....

....

....

....

....

....

....

....

....

....

....

....

....

....

....

What function does my eating disorder serve for me?

⪻⪼⪻⪼⪻⪼

All eating disorders exist for a reason. Perhaps your eating disorder helps you to feel in control, numb your emotions or show people that you are in pain. Have a think about why your eating disorder has been helpful for you.

....

....

....

....

....

....

....

....

....

....

....

....

....

....

....

....

....

....

How are you feeling today? Draw or write it out!

The power of music

Music can be an amazing tool for our wellbeing, and there are so many inspiring songs and artists out there. Making a motivational recovery playlist can be really useful when things feel tough – what songs would you put on yours?

Songs that make me feel motivated:

....

....

....

....

....

....

....

....

....

....

....

....

....

....

....

....

....

....

....

The real me

Something an eating disorder can be very good at is making us forget who we are as a person without it being there. Take some time to remind yourself of the real you underneath your eating disorder.

Who am I without my eating disorder?

....
....
....
....
....
....
....
....
....
....
....
....
....
....
....
....
....
....

The future me

We all have a future without an eating disorder, but it can be scary thinking about what that might look like. Have a think about who you would like to be in the future without having an eating disorder in your life.

Who would I like to be in the future?

....

....

....

....

....

....

....

....

....

....

....

....

....

....

....

....

....

....

....

....

Lies my eating disorder tells me

Eating disorders can be incredibly sneaky – let's have a think about some of the lies your eating disorder tells you.

1. ....
   ....

2. ....
   ....

3. ....
   ....

4. ....
   ....

5. ....
   ....

6. ....
   ....

7. ....
   ....

8. ....
   ....

9. ....
   ....

10. ....
    ....

Motivational placemats

Something that can be really useful to keep you motivated is to create something visual that you can use at the dining table, or wherever it is you eat your meals.

It can be a good activity to create your own placemat to use at the dinner table. You could include inspirational quotes, the reasons you are in recovery or photos of things that keep you motivated.

Once you are done, you can laminate the placemat and use it at every meal to keep you focussed on your goals and on the right track.

What could you include on your placemat? Use this space to brainstorm.

....
....
....
....
....
....
....
....
....
....
....
....
....
....
....
....

Things I hate about my eating disorder

1. ....
....

2. ....
....

3. ....
....

4. ....
....

5. ....
....

6. ....
....

7. ....
....

8. ....
....

9. ....
....

10. ....
....

What does my eating disorder stop me from doing?

1. ....
....

2. ....
....

3. ....
....

4. ....
....

5. ....
....

6. ....
....

7. ....
....

8. ....
....

9. ....
....

10. ....
....

Brain dump

How are you feeling right now? Sometimes getting our thoughts out onto the page can help us to process and make sense of them.

....

....

....

....

....

....

....

....

....

....

....

....

....

....

....

....

....

....

....

....

My skills and strengths

We all have different strengths that, if channelled in the right way, can be our greatest weapons against our eating disorder. What are some of your strengths and skills that you can use to fight your eating disorder's voice?

1. ....

....

2. ....

....

3. ....

....

4. ....

....

5. ....

....

6. ....

....

7. ....

....

8. ....

....

9. ....

....

10. ....

....

How are you feeling today? Draw or write it out!

Self-care activities

Eating disorders can make us be unkind to ourselves, and one of the greatest ways of fighting back against them is to start showing our minds and bodies some kindness. What self-care activities can you try?

1. ....
....

2. ....
....

3. ....
....

4. ....
....

5. ....
....

6. ....
....

7. ....
....

8. ....
....

9. ....
....

10. ....
....

People who help me

Living with an eating disorder can be a very isolating experience, and reaching out to people can make the world of difference. Make a list of some people who can help you; this could include family, friends, mental health services or charities, for example.

Family:

....

....

....

....

Friends:

....

....

....

....

Other:

....

....

....

....

Unhelpful thinking traps

Most of us have thinking habits developed over our lives that can sometimes get in the way when we are feeling distressing and difficult emotions. These are some of the most common ones that people experience.

Mind reading:

This is where we assume that we know what other people are thinking. Often we might be worrying what they are thinking about us.

Prediction:

Prediction is when we think we know what's going to happen in the future, and usually we are worrying about negative outcomes.

Comparing and despairing:

This is when we focus on the positives in others, but only see the negatives in ourselves.

Catastrophizing:

This is where we find ourselves believing or imagining that only the worst outcome is going to come true.

Mental filter:

Filtering is where we only notice what we want to, and subsequently filter out everything else that doesn't fit that narrative, like sieving out all the positives and only letting the negatives through.

Mountains and molehills:

This is where we exaggerate and focus on the negatives and minimize or ignore the positives.

Critical self:

We might have our critical self hat on when we are putting ourselves down and blaming ourselves for things that are not our fault.

Shoulds and musts:

This is when we put a lot of pressure on ourselves and have unreasonable or unrealistic expectations of what we should or shouldn't be doing.

Black and white thinking:

You might have your black and white thinking trap activated if you are only able to see things as good or bad, right or wrong, with no grey area in between.

Evaluations/judgements:

This is where we find ourselves making judgements about things instead of looking over the evidence we have in front of us.

Emotional reasoning:

This is where we assume that our feelings are always rational and proportionate to the situation. Remember, feelings are not facts.

Memories:

You might have your memories thinking trap activated when you are remembering distressing things that have happened and believing that the situation is happening in the present rather than in the past.

Everybody has their own individual traps – you might find some of these don't apply to you at all and others make complete sense. It might be helpful to think about which of them feel relevant to you, and situations where you think they might arise. For example, if you find yourself feeling very anxious about things that could happen in the future, you might be "catastrophizing" or "predicting". The more you start to recognize your own thinking traps, the more you can start to challenge them.

What are my unhelpful thinking traps?

When might I notice them?

How are you feeling today? Draw or write it out!

Brain dump

How are you feeling right now? Sometimes getting our thoughts out onto the page can help us to process and make sense of them.

....

....

....

....

....

....

....

....

....

....

....

....

....

....

....

....

....

....

....

....

Positive words wordsearch

The first three words you see are your words of the day.

N	N	O	U	R	I	S	H	S	N	P	P	E	F
O	C	O	A	B	R	A	V	E	P	E	A	B	L
S	P	O	S	I	T	I	V	I	T	Y	C	H	Y
E	E	P	C	A	O	A	F	C	P	T	E	G	P
E	P	M	P	I	F	I	F	L	A	P	A	N	L
F	H	A	C	C	E	P	T	A	N	C	E	I	E
E	C	A	G	C	U	U	V	F	E	E	E	H	A
C	C	C	P	N	E	I	A	E	P	A	V	S	I
A	P	A	E	P	I	T	S	N	P	P	O	I	L
L	E	G	O	V	I	L	P	A	O	E	L	R	I
M	E	R	N	L	I	N	A	E	S	L	F	U	A
A	R	I	I	E	N	E	E	E	R	E	L	O	P
M	A	F	I	L	M	P	I	S	H	B	E	L	A
T	P	E	A	C	E	F	U	L	S	U	S	F	H

ACCEPTANCE   HAPPINESS   BRAVE

SELF LOVE   FLOURISHING   POSITIVITY

CALM   HEALING

PEACEFUL   NOURISH

Communicating with others

Eating disorders can feel like they help us to manage our distress (though they do increase it in the long term). They can be very secretive, or we can use them as a way to communicate to others that we are struggling without having to tell them. This can make it difficult for people to help us, because they either don't know we are feeling this distress as we are keeping it a secret, or they are having to support us with the eating disorder symptoms first.

There are a lot of different ways we can let people know we are finding things difficult. This could be writing a letter to them, having code words or scheduling in regular check-ups, for example.

How could you communicate how you are feeling with people, without turning to your eating disorder to manage those difficult feelings?

....
....
....
....
....
....
....
....
....
....
....
....
....
....
....

What does my future look like without an eating disorder?

⊱⊱⊱⊱⊱⊱⊱⊱⊱⊰⊰⊰⊰⊰⊰⊰⊰⊰

What does my future look like with an eating disorder?

Coping statements

When we are anxious or upset, it can feel like those feelings are going to last forever. Here are some things you can say to yourself to get you through those moments.

I've done this before – I can do it again.

When this is over, I'll be glad I did it.

This seems hard now, but it will get easier with time.

Feelings are not facts.

I am moving forward all the time.

I can be anxious but still focus on what I need to be doing.

My feelings are not always rational – I am going to be okay.

Brain dump

How are you feeling right now? Sometimes getting our thoughts out onto the page can help us to process and make sense of them.

Recovery fears

Recovery is scary, there's no getting around that. It involves challenging some very difficult thoughts and feelings and sometimes it can feel easier not to do this, but it's important to remember that the more you challenge them the easier it gets. Have a think about what some of your biggest fears about recovery are, and how you can challenge them.

....

....

....

....

....

....

....

....

....

....

....

....

....

....

....

....

....

....

A goodbye letter to my eating disorder

Breaking up with our eating disorder can feel like we are saying goodbye to a part of our identity. However, there is so much more to you than this. It's okay to grieve; you are saying goodbye to a big part of your life. Try writing a goodbye letter to your eating disorder to help you process letting it go.

....

....

....

....

....

....

....

....

....

....

....

....

....

....

....

....

....

....

54321 grounding technique

Anxiety and distress can feel completely overwhelming sometimes. If you find yourself feeling like this, this technique can be very effective at bringing you back into the here and now by helping you to connect to your senses. There are five steps to follow.

1. Look around you and notice **five things you can see**. This could be a painting, a plant or a person, for example. Pay attention to what each of these things looks like: their shape, colour and size.

2. Focus on **four things you can feel**. This could be the wind, your clothes against your skin, the floor underneath your feet. Notice the different textures and sensations.

3. Name **three things you can hear**. Maybe there are birds chirping outside, or cars passing in the street. Perhaps you can hear a TV show in the background. Focus on the different tones and volumes.

4. Notice **two things you can smell**. Have you used a nice fabric softener on your clothes, or are you wearing your favourite perfume? Maybe you are outdoors and can smell plants and flowers.

5. Think about **one thing you can taste**. Perhaps you have chewing gum or a cup of tea nearby. If you can't taste anything, try to imagine the taste of one of your favourite things.

What is important to me and what do I value?

Eating disorders are often very all consuming and can make us feel detached from our values and the things we care about. It can be helpful when we are trying to recover to reconnect to some of our values to remind us why we are on this journey.

....

....

....

....

....

....

....

....

....

....

....

....

....

....

....

....

....

....

What does my life look like with an eating disorder?

Eating disorders can take up huge amounts of time and energy and can ultimately get in the way of a lot of other things in our life that are important to us. Think of this circle as being your life right now. If you were to divide it into a pie chart, how much of that would be your eating disorder, and how much would be left for everything else – work, friends, hobbies? For example, maybe your eating disorder is taking up 80% of your energy and thoughts right now. Doing this exercise can help motivate us to make changes, so that the pie chart of our lives can be full of the things we care about and value.

What does my life look like without an eating disorder?

Now think about what the pie chart of your life would look like if your eating disorder wasn't there. How much time would you like to dedicate to things you enjoy? Perhaps you'd like to spend a quarter of your life at work and a lot more of it socializing. Maybe you love studying and want to spend a third of your time doing that. If travelling is your goal, it might take up most of your circle. This is your individual pie chart, and it should align with your own goals and values.

How are you feeling today? Draw or write it out!

When you feel like giving up, remember why you started

Brain dump

How are you feeling right now? Sometimes getting our thoughts out onto the page can help us to process and make sense of them.

....

....

....

....

....

....

....

....

....

....

....

....

....

....

....

....

....

....

....

What would I say to a friend if they were going through this?

We are often able to be thoughtful and kind towards others but struggle to apply this to ourselves. Try thinking about what you'd say to somebody you care about if they were struggling with an eating disorder.

....

....

....

....

....

....

....

....

....

....

....

....

....

....

....

....

....

....

....

A letter to your younger self

When you were younger you probably didn't imagine that you would have an eating disorder in your future. If you could write a letter to your younger self, what would you say?

....

....

....

....

....

....

....

....

....

....

....

....

....

....

....

....

....

....

....

....

A letter to your future self

It might be difficult to envision your future without an eating disorder right now, but you owe it to your future self to recover. If you could write a letter to yourself in the future, what would you say?

....

....

....

....

....

....

....

....

....

....

....

....

....

....

....

....

....

....

....

....

Pros and cons of change

Sometimes, you might feel that you don't want to recover. Lots of us who are going through this process feel this way at times. This exercise is helpful to remind you why you have started this journey.

What are the pros of recovering?

....

....

....

What are the cons of recovering?

....

....

....

What are the pros of not recovering?

....

....

....

What are the cons of not recovering?

....

....

....

It's a beautiful day
to choose recovery

Letters to your eating disorder

All eating disorders serve a purpose, however difficult they are to live with. It can be a useful exercise to write letters to your eating disorder, one as if it is your friend and one as if it is your enemy. This can help you recognize what function it serves for you, but also why you want to move away from it and recover.

Try thinking about the ways your eating disorder has been helpful for you across your life, as well as all the things it has taken away from you.

To my eating disorder, my friend:

....

....

....

....

....

....

....

....

....

....

....

....

....

....

....

To my eating disorder, my enemy:

....

....

....

....

....

....

....

....

....

....

....

....

....

....

....

....

....

....

....

....

....

....

....

....

31 days of self-love

Each month, try to complete these activities to improve your self-esteem.

1 Write down one thing you like about your appearance	2 Forgive yourself	3 Think about an area where you need to set boundaries
8 What would you say to your inner child?	9 Write down three reasons you want to recover	10 Have a social media detox day
15 Think about one way you make the world a better place	16 Think of one change you need to make to increase your happiness	17 List three of your role models and the qualities you admire in them
22 Find three motivational quotes that mean something to you	23 Think of something nice you have done for someone recently	24 Tell somebody you love them
29 Write down something you have done well today	30 Think about the last positive thing somebody said about you	31 Take five minutes to have a cup of tea

4 Write down three things you like about your personality	5 Do a self-care activity	6 Say yes to something	7 List three things that make you happy to be alive
11 Think about what your younger self would be proud of you for	12 Reach out to a friend	13 Listen to an uplifting song	14 Do five minutes of relaxation or mindfulness
18 Think of three positive words other people would use to describe you	19 Make a list of all your achievements today	20 Declutter and tidy your safe space	21 Eat something nourishing
25 Think about the last time you did something nice for somebody	26 Make a choice today that your future self would be grateful for	27 Take half an hour to read a book	28 Wear your favourite outfit

GREAT THINGS NEVER COME FROM COMFORT ZONES

How are you feeling today? Draw or write it out!

What does recovery mean to you?

Recovery looks different for everybody; it can be useful to think about what your personal version of recovery looks like.

Daily positive affirmations

It might feel counter-intuitive when you're having a bad day, and you might not always believe what you are saying, but it can help to have some daily positive affirmations. Try repeating these to yourself each day.

People like me for who I am

My feelings are important

I matter

I am allowed to take up space

I am not perfect and that's okay

I deserve good things

My body is my home

I am worthy of the love people give me

I am good enough as I am

It's a good day to have a good day

People who inspire me

We can draw inspiration from lots of different places, but sometimes having people we look up to can be really helpful. Who inspires you to recover?

1. ....
....

2. ....
....

3. ....
....

4. ....
....

5. ....
....

6. ....
....

7. ....
....

8. ....
....

9. ....
....

10. ....
....

How are you feeling today? Draw or write it out!

Square breathing technique

Square breathing has been shown to be helpful when experiencing high anxiety and is an exercise that can be used wherever you are. Find a window, a wall, a painting or any other square shape you can see to focus on. If you can't see one, you can use your index finger to trace one in front of you.

Slowly trace your eyes across the top of the square in front of you, breathing in for a count of four. As you scan down the right side of the square, hold your breath for a count of four. Breathe out for a count of four as you trace the bottom of the square, then hold for a count of four as you scan up the left-hand side. Repeat this as many times as necessary, breathing in a slow and controlled way.

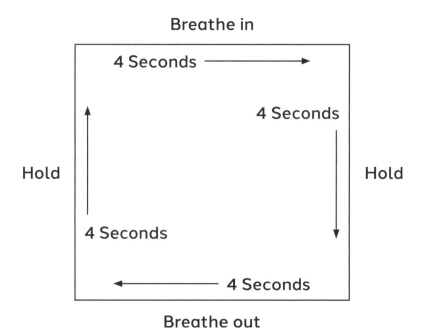

What are my triggers?

We all have triggers that can lead to lapses and relapses, and make recovery feel more difficult. Writing them down can help us to recognize them, so we can then learn to challenge and cope with them when they arise.

Once we have identified triggers, we can start to notice them more. The world can be a difficult place at times and sometimes we are going to come across things that trigger us.

....

....

....

....

....

....

....

....

....

....

....

....

....

....

....

....

....

....

20 affirmations to improve body image

The problem is not your body, it's how you feel about it

There is no such thing as a perfect body

No one cares about your weight as much as you do

You might not like your legs, but they take you places

Life is too short to waste time obsessing about your body

Photos we see in the media are not reality

Happiness isn't a number

You can love yourself without liking everything about yourself

Your weight is not your worth

Don't value your body over your being

You are allowed to take up space

Hating your body will never lead to happiness

Your body keeps you alive and deserves care and respect

Don't let your mind bully your body

Your body is an instrument, not an ornament

You have to nourish to flourish

You can't hate yourself into a version of yourself that you love

Your body is important and you deserve to take care of it

You are not alive just to pay bills and lose weight

How much you weigh is the least interesting thing about you

Affirmations jar

Similar to the "quote jar" earlier, writing down positive body image affirmations and reading them every day can help us to improve our self-esteem. Try writing down some of the phrases on the previous pages and taking one out every day, or when you need a reminder to appreciate your body.

It can also be helpful to write these down and stick them around mirrors in your house, as this may be somewhere where you find yourself judging your body the most.

Brain dump

How are you feeling right now? Sometimes getting our thoughts out onto the page can help us to process and make sense of them.

How to get through bad body image days

Our relationships with our bodies are complicated and some days, no matter how much we try, we can't get past our struggles with our body image. Here are some strategies to help get through those days. Remind yourself why you are recovering:

Go back to your reasons to recover, look at your motivational poster, envision your life without an eating disorder.

Use body neutral comments:

"I have a body", "My body does xyz"

Remind yourself why your body is amazing:

Think of all the things it does for you.

Use distractions:

Try and do some activities you enjoy – maybe go back to the list you wrote earlier on in this book.

Don't isolate yourself:

Speak to a friend or somebody you care about.

Do something kind for yourself:

Practise self-care activities.

Miracle question

If you woke up tomorrow and your eating disorder was completely gone, what would your day look like?

....

....

....

....

....

....

....

....

....

....

....

....

....

....

....

....

....

....

....

....

My favourite memories

We can be so mean when talking to and about our bodies, but they have carried us through life. Try thinking about some of your favourite memories and the role your body has played in making them happen.

....

....

....

....

....

....

....

....

....

....

....

....

....

....

....

....

....

....

....

What do I like about my body?

This is a very difficult question for a lot of people to answer, and you may feel like you can't come up with an answer at all. If that's the case, try to think of part of your body that you feel neutrally towards.

....

....

....

....

....

....

....

....

....

....

....

....

....

....

....

....

....

....

....

....

What does my body do for me?

Something that can be really helpful when thinking about our bodies is not to focus on what they look like, but instead appreciate what they do. Have a think about the part of your body that you dislike the most and what its function is. Then think about all the things you can do and have done because of that part of your body. Do this for three more parts of your body.

Body part: ....

What does it do/what is its function?

....

....

....

What does it allow me to do?

....

....

....

Body part: ....

What does it do/what is its function?

....

....

....

What does it allow me to do?

....

....

....

Body part: . . . .

What does it do/what is its function?

. . . .

. . . .

. . . .

What does it allow me to do?

. . . .

. . . .

. . . .

Body part: . . . .

What does it do/what is its function?

. . . .

. . . .

. . . .

What does it allow me to do?

. . . .

. . . .

. . . .

You were born
to be real, not to
be perfect

How are you feeling today? Draw or write it out!

Who am I to others?

We've thought about who we are from our own perspective, but it can also be really useful to think about who we are to other people. Ask those around you how they would describe you – some of the answers might surprise you.

....

....

....

....

....

....

....

....

....

....

....

....

....

....

....

....

....

....

....

Brain dump

How are you feeling right now? Sometimes getting our thoughts out onto the page can help us to process and make sense of them.

....

....

....

....

....

....

....

....

....

....

....

....

....

....

....

....

....

....

....

....

What does your eating disorder look like?

Try drawing it below.

What does your eating disorder say?

We've drawn what it looks like, but what sort of things does it say to you?

....

....

....

....

....

....

....

....

....

....

....

....

....

....

....

....

....

....

....

Coping with guilt

Going against what your eating disorder wants can often provoke lots of feelings of guilt or shame. The most important thing to remember is that the more you challenge it, the less guilt and shame you will feel, but this does take time. To help you cope with these feelings, try to remind yourself the reasons why you are going against what your eating disorder is telling you. Think about what you would say to a friend if they were in the same situation. Remind yourself that you are worthy and deserving of recovery, take some deep breaths, and be kind to yourself until the feeling passes. It will pass, even when it feels like it won't.

How are you feeling today? Draw or write it out!

How to make a self-soothe box

Self-soothe boxes, also referred to as crisis boxes or sensory boxes, are excellent tools to have access to. They are designed to be full of items that help you to get through periods of distress. Try to fill yours with things that cater to each of your five senses. Here are some suggestions of things you could include that might be helpful.

- ❀ **Taste:** Chocolates or mints, or maybe your favourite tea bags

- ❀ **Smell:** Essential oils, nice hand creams or perfume

- ❀ **Touch:** Stress balls, tangles or something soft like a small cuddly toy

- ❀ **Hear:** A prompt card to remind you to access your happy playlist or favourite song

- ❀ **See:** Photos of people you love, motivational quotes or perhaps some letters of encouragement

It might also be helpful to keep a list of distractions, helplines or apps that you find useful when you are finding things difficult.

What will go in my self-soothe box?

....

....

....

....

....

....

....

....

What can the people around me do to help?

People often want to help those they care about but aren't always sure how. What could those around you do that would be helpful for your recovery, and what do they do that is unhelpful?

Helpful:

....

....

....

....

....

....

....

....

Unhelpful:

....

....

....

....

....

....

....

....

Brain dump

How are you feeling right now? Sometimes getting our thoughts out onto the page can help us to process and make sense of them.

....

....

....

....

....

....

....

....

....

....

....

....

....

....

....

....

....

....

....

....

....

Challenge jars

Creating a "challenge jar" can be a good way to keep you accountable. For some people these could be challenging different foods, for others different compensatory behaviours. Make a list of what you would put in your jar then try taking one out each week to try. Sometimes we may have to face a challenge more than once for it to feel easier, so if you need to put it back in the jar to try again later, that's okay.

1. ....
   ....

2. ....
   ....

3. ....
   ....

4. ....
   ....

5. ....
   ....

6. ....
   ....

7. ....
   ....

8. ....
   ....

9. ....
   ....

10. ....
    ....

How are you feeling today? Draw or write it out!

How to stay motivated

It's normal for motivation to fluctuate in recovery. Here are some questions you can ask yourself to help you to stay on track.

What are my long-term goals?

....

....

....

What changes do I need to make to reach these goals?

....

....

....

How would making these changes improve things?

....

....

....

How would the last week have gone differently if I'd made these changes?

....

....

....

What am I most worried about?

....

....

....

Who can I use for support?

....

....

....

Ways I can stay motivated:

1. ....

    ....

2. ....

    ....

3. ....

    ....

4. ....

    ....

5. ....

    ....

6. ....

    ....

My eating disorder rules

Eating disorders often impose a lot of rules on us, which can feel very anxiety provoking to go against. These can include food groups we avoid, what times we eat, where we eat and how much exercise we do, for example. It can feel like going against these rules is completely impossible sometimes; however, the more times we challenge a rule, the easier it gets.

Have a think about some of your eating disorder rules, and what it is about them that makes them feel scary to challenge.

What is the rule?

....

....

Why is it scary to break?

....

....

How can I challenge it?

....

....

What is the rule?

....

....

Why is it scary to break?

....

....

How can I challenge it?

....

....

What is the rule?

....

....

Why is it scary to break?

....

....

How can I challenge it?

....

....

What is the rule?

....

....

Why is it scary to break?

....

....

How can I challenge it?

....

....

My fear foods

Lots of people with eating disorders have foods that feel really scary for them, and also foods that feel "safe". It is important to challenge the foods that scare us, as this will enable us to have more freedom in the future. Challenging fear foods can be very difficult. Some people find they want to go straight in with the things they are most anxious about, but others like to build up to the hardest ones slowly. Have a think about the foods that worry you the most, and then we can start to think about how we can challenge them.

Foods I fear the least	Foods I fear a bit	Foods I fear the most

Overcoming fear foods

1. Ask yourself why you are afraid of this food or what purpose the rule serves for you.

2. Write down every reason you are afraid, and for every one list a reason why you should challenge yourself.

3. Plan when you are going to do this challenge, and maybe let someone else know to help hold you accountable.

4. Tell your eating disorder to go away and remind yourself that you are in control.

5. Use things around you that can help, like your placemat, or write some of your goals down to focus on.

6. Repeat until it is not a fear food or a rule any more (you might have to do this lots of times!).

Safety behaviours

Safety behaviours are things we do to help lower our anxiety in challenging situations. For people with eating disorders, this might include only eating with certain cutlery, picking the same brands of food or avoiding having certain foods in the house. Everyone's safety behaviours are individual to them. The problem with these behaviours is that although they make us less anxious in the short term, in the long run they keep us stuck. For example, if we only ever eat off the same plate, we never give ourselves a chance to learn that nothing bad happens if we eat from a different plate.

Try having a think about what some of your safety behaviours are, and how you can start to challenge them.

Safety behaviour: ....

....

....

How can I challenge this?

....

....

....

Safety behaviour: ....

....

....

How can I challenge this?

....

....

....

Safety behaviour: . . . .

. . . .

. . . .

How can I challenge this?

. . . .

. . . .

. . . .

Safety behaviour: . . . .

. . . .

. . . .

How can I challenge this?

. . . .

. . . .

. . . .

Safety behaviour: . . . .

. . . .

. . . .

How can I challenge this?

. . . .

. . . .

. . . .

You are enough
You always have been
You always will be

Brain dump

How are you feeling right now? Sometimes getting our thoughts out onto the page can help us to process and make sense of them.

....

....

....

....

....

....

....

....

....

....

....

....

....

....

....

....

....

....

....

....

My traffic lights

Sometimes it can be helpful to think of our progress and recovery in terms of a traffic light system: red meaning relapse, orange meaning we need to be careful and pay more attention to our thoughts and behaviours, and green meaning we are well and happy. Have a think about what life looks like for you in each of these zones and what your plan of action would be for each one.

What does my green zone look like?

....

....

How can I stay in this zone?

....

....

What does my orange zone look like?

....

....

How can I get out of this zone?

....

....

What does my red zone look like?

....

....

How can I get out of this zone?

....

....

Staying well

There are lots of things we need to do to keep ourselves on track, some every day and some less often. Have a think about what some of these are for you.

What can I do on a daily basis to keep myself well?

....

....

....

....

....

What can I do on a weekly basis to keep myself well?

....

....

....

....

....

What do I need to do monthly or less often to keep myself well?

....

....

....

....

....

Letter writing

Another letter-writing exercise that can be helpful is to write to our body, thanking it for what it has done for us and apologizing to it for what we have put it through. What would you say to your body?

....

....

....

....

....

....

....

....

....

....

....

....

....

....

....

....

....

....

....

....

....

Managing setbacks

Eating disorders are coping mechanisms, and it's likely we are all going to have things that happen in our lives that require us to use our coping skills, whatever those may be. Have a think about what might lead to a setback for you, and how you would manage it.

What could cause a setback?

....

....

....

....

....

....

....

....

How could I manage this?

....

....

....

....

....

....

....

....

Brain dump

How are you feeling right now? Sometimes getting our thoughts out onto the page can help us to process and make sense of them.

....

....

....

....

....

....

....

....

....

....

....

....

....

....

....

....

....

....

....

....

What have I achieved since starting this journal?

I hope that over the time you have been working through this book, you have been able to start challenging your eating disorder. What are some of the things you have achieved, no matter how big or small, since you started using this journal?

....

....

....

....

....

....

....

....

....

....

....

....

....

....

....

....

....

....

Congratulations, fighter!

You've worked your way through this recovery journal. I hope that you have found some of these exercises useful and that they have got you thinking about your eating disorder and why you want to recover.

There are some other excellent resources out there to help you on your journey; you can find some of these at the back of the book.

I wish you all the luck in the world for your continued recovery. Remember, there is so much more to life than existing with an eating disorder, and you are worthy, deserving and capable of living it.

Lots of love, Cara

Useful Resources

Websites and helplines

Beat (UK): www.beateatingdisorders.org.uk / 0808 801 0677
NEDA (US): www.nationaleatingdisorders.org / 1800 931 2237
NEDIC (Canada): www.nedic.ca / 416 340 4156
EDANZ (New Zealand): www.ed.org.nz / 0800 233 269
Butterfly (Australia): www.butterfly.org.au / 1800 33 4673

Books that I've found helpful

Crabbe, M.J. (2017) *Body Positive Power: How to Stop Dieting, Make Peace with Your Body and Live.* London: Vermilion.

Davis, Dr N. and Baker, E. (2016) *Eating Disorder Recovery Handbook: A Practical Guide to Long-Term Recovery.* London: Jessica Kingsley Publishers.

Farrar, T. (2019) *Rehabilitate, Rewire, Recover: Anorexia Recovery for the Determined Adult.* Independently published.

Freeman, L. (2019) *The Reading Cure: How Books Restored My Appetite.* London: Weidenfeld & Nicolson.

Sandoz, E. (2014) *Living with Your Body and Other Things You Hate.* Oakland, CA: New Harbinger.

Tandoh, R. (2018) *Eat Up: Food, Appetite and Eating What You Want.* London: Serpent's Tail.

Thomas, L. (2019) *Just Eat It: How Intuitive Eating Can Help You Get Your Shit Together Around Food.* London: Bluebird.

Treasure, J., Smith, G. and Crane, A. (2016) *Skills-Based Caring for a Loved One with an Eating Disorder: The New Maudsley Method* (2nd edn). Abingdon/New York: Routledge.

Acknowledgements

There are so many people to thank for the role they have played in my recovery, without which my progress and subsequently this book wouldn't have been possible.

Thank you to Leigh House, who as a child gave me some respite from my eating disorder and taught me that I had the potential to grow and progress in life, as well as inspiring my future career.

Thank you to April House, who over the course of my adulthood have never given up hope, and have always made me believe there is more to life and more to who I am than anorexia.

And most of all, thank you to my partner, my best friends and my family for standing by me no matter what, and reminding me every day why I want to recover.

About the Author

Cara Lisette has struggled with anorexia nervosa since her early teens and has had treatment in inpatient, day patient and outpatient services. It is through each of these recovery journeys that she has learnt many different skills and strategies to help challenge her eating disorder, and most recently discovered the value of journalling her way through recovery. She put this book together in the hope that some of the things she has found helpful throughout her own journey can also be helpful for others. She runs a successful blog (www.car-as-corner.com) about her experiences with eating disorders and can be found on Twitter and Instagram at @caralisette, where you can follow her recovery journey in more detail and keep up to date with her other projects. She is also a qualified cognitive behavioural therapist and registered mental health nurse so, in addition to her lived experience of having an eating disorder, she has also brought her professional skills and knowledge to this book.

of related interest

Eating Disorder Recovery Handbook
A Practical Guide to Long-Term Recovery
Dr Nicola Davies and Emma Bacon
ISBN 978 1 78592 133 9
eISBN 978 1 78450 398 7

I Can Beat Anorexia!
Finding the Motivation, Confidence and Skills to Recover and Avoid Relapse
Dr Nicola Davies
ISBN 978 1 78592 187 2
eISBN 978 1 78450 459 5

Weight Expectations
One Man's Recovery from Anorexia
Dave Chawner
ISBN 978 1 78592 358 6
eISBN 978 1 78450 699 5

The Recovery Mama Guide to Your Eating Disorder
Recovery in Pregnancy and Postpartum
Linda Shanti McCabe
Foreword by Carolyn Costin
ISBN 978 1 78592 829 1
eISBN 978 1 78592 590 0

Maintaining Recovery from Eating Disorders
Avoiding Relapse and Recovering Life
Naomi Feigenbaum
Foreword by Rebekah Bardwell
ISBN 978 1 84905 815 5
eISBN 978 0 85700 250 1